AF594220

A SHAKESPEARE TREASURY

WILLIAM SHAKESPEARE

Born 1564. *Died* 1616.

A SHAKESPEARE TREASURY

Selected by
LEVI FOX
Director Emeritus of the Shakespeare Birthplace Trust

JARROLD PUBLISHING

Lines of fair comfort and encouragement . . .
King Richard the Third, Act 5, Sc. 2.

Let me hear a staff, a stanze, a verse . . .
Love's Labour's Lost, Act 4, Sc. 2.

He hath songs for man or woman, of all sizes . . .
The Winter's Tale, Act 4, Sc. 4.

I have a sonnet that will serve the turn . . .
The Two Gentlemen of Verona, Act 3, Sc. 2.

ISBN 0-85306-946-8
ISBN 0-85306-947-6 (satin bound)

Jarrold Publishing, Norwich
Printed in Great Britain

PREFACE

THIS is essentially a personal anthology, an offering of select passages from Shakespeare's works which over the years have given me pleasure, inspiration and comfort. As Director of the Shakespeare Birthplace Trust for more than forty years it was my fortunate responsibility to have in my care Shakespeare's Birthplace – probably the world's most famous literary Mecca – and to find myself much involved with the educational and academic activities associated with the important library, archives and museum collections in my custody. In so doing I not only came to appreciate the infinite variety and richness of Shakespeare's works, but also to realise in what universal esteem his genius is held by people of all nationalities. Indeed, though an Englishman, Shakespeare belongs to the world. In him we have a man who speaks with authority as clearly and convincingly today as he did in the adventurous and uncertain times when he lived.

I have called my selection a treasury because it contains good and precious things. Many of the passages of verse included are already well known and have been frequently printed and quoted; among them are some of the most beautiful and famous verse compositions in the English language. Others are not so familiar but are equally illustrative of Shakespeare's remarkable knowledge and understanding of every conceivable subject and facet of human character, not to mention of his incomparable mastery of language and poetic verse.

Ideally the passages should be read in the context of the plays or poems from which they are taken, but for convenience of reference I have added titles which seem appropriate. So far as arrangement is concerned no attempt has been made to follow any pattern or theme. The resultant medley with its mixture of ingredients should therefore provide reading for all occasions, moods and situations, both for young and old. At the same time I venture to hope that some readers will feel moved to become better acquainted with that even greater treasury of wisdom and beauty – the Complete Works of Shakespeare himself.

LEVI FOX

The Shakespeare Centre
Stratford-upon-Avon

CONTENTS

BEN JONSON'S EULOGY

To draw no envy (Shakespeare) on thy name,
Am I thus ample to thy Book and Fame:
While I confess thy writings to be such
As neither Man nor Muse can praise too much . . .
Soule of the Age!
The applause! delight! the wonder of our Stage! . . .
Thou art a Monument without a tomb,
And art alive still while thy Book doth live
And we have wits to read and praise to give.

Preface to the First Folio edition of Shakespeare's works, 1623.

POETIC POWER

Say that upon the altar of her beauty
You sacrifice your tears, your sighs, your
heart.
Write till your ink be dry, and with your
tears
Moist it again, and frame some feeling line
That may discover such integrity:
For Orpheus' lute was strung with poets'
sinews,
Whose golden touch could soften steel and
stones,
Make tigers tame and huge leviathans
Forsake unsounded deeps to dance on
sands.

The Two Gentlemen of Verona, Act 3, Sc. 2.

YOUNG LOVE

Tell me where is fancy bred,
Or in the heart or in the head,
How begot, how nourished?
    Reply, reply.
It is engend'red in the eyes,
With gazing fed; and fancy dies
In the cradle where it lies.
    Let us all ring fancy's knell:
    I'll begin it – Ding, dong, bell.
    Ding, dong, bell.

The Merchant of Venice, Act 3, Sc. 2.

THE PLAYERS

Good my lord, will you see the players well bestowed? Do you hear, let them be well used; for they are the abstracts and brief chronicles of the time: after your death you were better have a bad epitaph than their ill report while you live.

Hamlet, Act 2, Sc. 2.

THE ACTOR'S ART

As in a theatre, the eyes of men,
After a well-grac'd actor leaves the stage,
Are idly bent on him that enters next,
Thinking his prattle to be tedious.

King Richard the Second, Act 5, Sc. 2.

Life's but a walking shadow, a poor
player
That struts and frets his hour upon the
stage,
And then is heard no more.

Macbeth, Act 5, Sc. 5.

Like a dull actor now,
I have forgot my part, and I am out,
Even to a full disgrace.

Coriolanus, Act 5, Sc. 3.

HOUSE-BUILDING

When we mean to build,
We first survey the plot, then draw the model;
And when we see the figure of the house,
Then must we rate the cost of the erection;
Which if we find outweighs ability,
What do we then but draw anew the model
In fewer offices, or at least desist
To build at all? Much more, in this great work, –
Which is almost to pluck a kingdom down
And set another up, – should we survey
The plot of situation and the model,
Consent upon a sure foundation,
Question surveyors; . . .

King Henry the Fourth, Pt. 2, Act 1, Sc. 3.

LUXURY

First, as you know, my house within the city
Is richly furnished with plate and gold:
Basins and ewers to lave her dainty hands;
My hangings all of Tyrian tapestry;
In ivory coffers I have stuff'd my crowns;
In cypress chests my arras counterpoints,
Costly apparel, tents, and canopies,
Fine linen, Turkey cushions boss'd with pearl,
Valance of Venice gold in needle-work,
Pewter and brass, and all things that belong
To house or housekeeping: then, at my farm
I have a hundred milch-kine to the pail,
Six score fat oxen standing in my stalls,
And all things answerable to this portion.

The Taming of the Shrew, Act 2, Sc. 1.

OPHELIA'S SONG

How should I your true love know
From another one?
'By his cockle hat and staff
And his sandal shoon.'

He is dead and gone, lady,
He is dead and gone;
At his head a grass-green turf,
At his heels a stone.

White his shroud as the mountain snow,
Larded with sweet flowers,
Which bewept to the grave did go
With true-love showers.

Hamlet, Act 4, Sc. 5.

O, MISTRESS MINE

O, Mistress mine, where are you roaming?
O, stay and hear; your true love's coming,
    That can sing both high and low;
Trip no further, pretty sweeting,
Journeys end in lovers meeting,
    Every wise man's son doth know.

What is love? 'tis not hereafter,
Present mirth hath present laughter,
    What's to come is still unsure:
In delay there lies no plenty,
Then come kiss me, sweet and twenty,
    Youth's a stuff will not endure.

Twelfth Night, Act 2, Sc. 3.

LOVE IS A SPIRIT

Bid me discourse, I will enchant thine ear,
Or like a fairy trip upon the green,
Or, like a nymph, with long dishevell'd
  hair,
Dance on the sands, and yet no footing
  seen:
Love is a spirit all compact of fire,
Not gross to sink, but light, and will aspire.

Venus and Adonis.

WHAT 'TIS TO LOVE

Good shepherd, tell this youth what 'tis to
  love.
It is to be all made of sighs and tears: –
It is to be all made of faith and service: –
It is to be all made of fantasy,
All made of passion, and all made of
  wishes;
All adoration, duty, and observance;
All humbleness, all patience, and
  impatience;
All purity, all trial, all obeisance;
And so am I for Phebe.

As You Like It, Act 5, Sc. 2.

MEMORY

When to the sessions of sweet silent thought
I summon up remembrance of things past,
I sigh the lack of many a thing I sought,
And with old woes new wail my dear time's waste.
Then can I drown an eye, unus'd to flow,
For precious friends hid in death's dateless night,
And weep afresh love's long since cancell'd woe,
And moan th' expense of many a vanish'd sight.
Then can I grieve at grievances foregone,
And heavily from woe to woe tell o'er
The sad account of fore-bemoaned moan,
Which I new pay as if not paid before.
But if the while I think on thee, dear friend,
All losses are restor'd, and sorrows end.

Sonnets, 30.

TIME

Like as the waves make towards the
pebbled shore,
So do our minutes hasten to their end;
Each changing place with that which goes
before
In sequent toil all forwards do contend.
Nativity, once in the main of light,
Crawls to maturity, wherewith being
crown'd,
Crooked eclipses 'gainst his glory fight,
And Time that gave doth now his gift
confound.
Time doth transfix the flourish set on youth,
And delves the parallels in beauty's brow,
Feeds on the rarities of nature's truth,
And nothing stands but for his scythe to mow.
And yet to times in hope my verse
shall stand,
Praising they worth, despite his cruel
hand.

Sonnets, 60.

NIGHT

Be innocent of the knowledge, dearest chuck,
Till thou applaud the deed. Come, seeling night,
Scarf up the tender eye of pitiful day,
And with thy bloody and invisible hand,
Cancel and tear to pieces that great bond
Which keeps me pale! Light thickens, and the crow
Makes wing to the rooky wood;
Good things of the day begin to droop and drowse,
Whiles night's black agents to their preys do rouse.

Macbeth, Act 3, Sc. 2.

SLEEP

Sleep that knits up the ravell'd sleave of care,
The death of each day's life, sore labour's bath,
Balm of hurt minds, great nature's second course,
Chief nourisher in life's feast.

Macbeth, Act 2, Sc. 2.

DOGS

Ay, in the catalogue ye go for men;
As hounds, and greyhounds, mongrels,
  spaniels, curs,
Shoughs, water-rugs, and demi-wolves,
  are clept
All by the name of dogs: the valu'd file
Distinguishes the swift, the slow, the subtle,
The housekeeper, the hunter.

Macbeth, Act 3, Sc. 1.

Mastiff, greyhound, mongrel grim,
Hound or spaniel, brach or lym,
Or bobtail tike, or trundletail.

King Lear, Act 3, Sc. 6.

ADONIS'S HORSE

Round-hoof'd, short-jointed, fetlocks
shag and long,
Broad breast, full eye, small head, and
nostril wide,
High crest, short ears, straight legs and
passing strong,
Thin mane, thick tail, broad buttock,
tender hide:
Look, what a horse should have he
did not lack,
Save a proud rider on so proud a back.

Venus and Adonis.

ORPHEUS WITH HIS LUTE

Orpheus with his lute made trees,
And the mountain-tops that freeze,
Bow themselves when he did sing.
To his music plants and flowers
Ever sprung, as sun and showers
There had made a lasting spring.

Everything that heard him play,
Even the billows of the sea,
Hung their heads, and then lay by.
In sweet music is such art,
Killing care and grief of heart
Fall asleep, or hearing die.

King Henry the Eighth, Act 3, Sc. 1.

OLIVIA

Make me a willow cabin at your gate,
And call upon my soul within the house;
Write loyal cantons of contemned love,
And sing them loud even in the dead of
  night;
Halloo your name to the reverberate hills,
And make the babbling gossip of the air
Cry out, 'Olivia'.

Twelfth Night, Act 1, Sc. 5.

IDYLLIC NATURE

When daisies pied and violets blue
And lady-smocks all silver-white
And cuckoo-buds of yellow hue
Do paint the meadows with delight,
The cuckoo then, on every tree,
Mocks married men, for thus sings he,
            Cuckoo;
Cuckoo, cuckoo: O, word of fear,
Unpleasing to a married ear!

Love's Labour's Lost, Act 5, Sc. 2.

A GARLAND OF SPRING

Now, my fairest friend,
I would I had some flowers of the spring that might
Become your time of day . . . daffodils,
That come before the swallow dares, and take
The winds of March with beauty; violets dim,
But sweeter than the lids of Juno's eyes
Or Cytherea's breath; pale primroses,
That die unmarried, ere they can behold
Bright Phoebus in his strength, a malady
Most incident to maids; bold oxlips and
The crown imperial; lilies of all kinds,
The flower-de-luce being one. O! these I lack
To make you garlands of, and my sweet friend,
To strew him o'er and o'er!

The Winter's Tale, Act 4, Sc. 4.

THE PEDLAR'S SONG

Will you buy any tape,
Or lace for your cape,
My dainty duck, my dear-a?
Any silk, any thread,
Any toys for your head,
Of the new'st and finest, finest wear-a?
Come to the pedlar;
Money's a meddler,
That doth utter all men's ware-a.

The Winter's Tale, Act 4, Sc. 3.

THE PEDLAR'S WARES

Lawn as white as driven snow,
Cypress black as e'er was crow,
Gloves as sweet as damask roses,
Masks for faces and for noses;
Bugle bracelet, necklace amber,
Perfume for a lady's chamber;
Golden quoifs and stomachers,
For my lads to give their dears,
Pins and poking-sticks of steel:
What maids lack from head to heel;
Come, buy of me, come! come buy, come
  buy!
Buy, lads or else your lasses cry.
Come buy!

The Winter's Tale, Act 4, Sc. 3.

THREE GLORIOUS SUNS

Three glorious suns, each one a perfect sun;
Not separated with the racking clouds,
But sever'd in a pale clear-shining sky.
See, see! they join, embrace, and seem to kiss,
As if they vow'd some league inviolable:
Now are they but one lamp, one light, one sun.
In this the heaven figures some event.

King Henry the Sixth, Pt 3, Act 2, Sc. 1.

HAIL, HEAVEN!

A goodly day not to keep house, with such
Whose roof's as low as ours! Stoop, boys: this gate
Instructs you how to adore the heavens; and bows you
To morning's holy office: the gates of monarchs
Are arch'd so high, that giants may jet through
And keep their impious turbans on, without
Good-morrow to the sun. – Hail, thou fair heaven!
We house i' the rock, yet use thee not so hardly
As prouder livers do.

Cymbeline, Act 3, Sc. 3.

THE APOTHECARY

And in his needy shop a tortoise hung,
An alligator stuff'd, and other skins
Of ill-shaped fishes; and about his shelves
A beggarly account of empty boxes,
Green earthen pots, bladders, and musty
  seeds,
Remnants of packthread, and old cakes of
  roses,
Were thinly scatter'd, to make up a show.

Romeo and Juliet, Act 5, Sc. 1.

THE DOCTOR

'Tis known, I ever
Have studied physic, through which secret art,
By turning o'er authorities, I have –
Together with my practice – made familiar
To me and to my aid the blest infusions
That dwell in vegetives, in metals, stones;
And I can speak of the disturbances
That nature works, and of her cures; which doth give me
A more content in course of true delight
Than to be thirsty after tottering honour,
Or tie my treasure up in silken bags,
To please the fool and death.

Pericles, Act 3, Sc. 2.

SHORTCOMINGS

The whips and scorns of time,
The oppressor's wrong, the proud man's
contumely,
The pangs of dispriz'd love, the law's
delay,
The insolence of office, and the spurns
That patient merit of the unworthy
takes. . . .

Hamlet, Act 3, Sc. 1.

FALSEHOOD

Mark you this, Bassanio,
The devil can cite Scripture for his purpose.
An evil soul, producing holy witness,
Is like a villain with a smiling cheek,
A goodly apple rotten at the heart:
O what a goodly outside falsehood hath!

The Merchant of Venice, Act 1, Sc. 3.

ORDER OF BATTLE

I will lead forth my soldiers to the plain,
And thus my battle shall be ordered:
My foreward shall be drawn out all in
  length
Consisting equally of horse and foot;
Our archers shall be placed in the midst.

Fight, gentlemen of England! fight, bold
  yeomen!
Draw, archers, draw your arrows to the
  head!
Spur your proud horses hard, and ride in
  blood;
Amaze the welkin with your broken
  staves!

King Richard the Third, Act 5, Sc. 3.

ONCE MORE UNTO THE BREACH

Once more unto the breach, dear friends, once more;
Or close the wall up with our English dead!
In peace there's nothing so becomes a man
As modest stillness and humility:
But when the blast of war blows in our ears,
Then imitate the action of the tiger;
Stiffen the sinews, summon up the blood,
Disguise fair nature with hard-favour'd rage;
Then lend the eye a terrible aspect.

King Henry the Fifth, Act 3, Sc. 1.

RUE, HERB OF GRACE

Poor Queen! so that thy state might be no worse
I would my skill were subject to thy curse –
Here did she drop a tear; here, in this place,
I'll set a bank of rue, sour herb of grace.
Rue, even for ruth, here shortly shall be seen,
In the remembrance of a weeping queen.

King Richard the Second, Act 3, Sc. 4.

A ROSE IS BEST

Of all flowers
Methinks a Rose is best.
It is the very emblem of a maid.
For when the west wind courts her gently.
How modestly she blows, and paints the
sun
With her chaste blushes. When the north
winds near her,
Rude and impatient, then like chastity,
She locks her beauties in her bud again,
And leaves him to base briers.

Two Noble Kinsmen, Act 2, Sc. 2.

CLEOPATRA TRIUMPHANT

For her own person,
It beggar'd all description; she did lie
In her pavilion, – cloth-of-gold of tissue, –
O'er-picturing that Venus where we see
The fancy outwork nature; on each side her
Stood pretty-dimpled boys, like smiling Cupids,
With divers-colour'd fans, whose wind did seem
To glow the delicate cheeks which they did cool,
And what they undid did.

Antony and Cleopatra, Act 2, Sc. 2.

YOUNG HARRY

I saw young Harry, with his beaver on,
His cuisses on his thighs, gallantly arm'd,
Rise from the ground like feather'd
Mercury,
And vaulted with such ease into his seat,
As if an angel dropp'd down from the
clouds,
To turn and wind a fiery Pegasus,
And witch the world with noble
horsemanship.

King Henry the Fourth, Pt 1, Act 4, Sc. 1.

HONOUR

Honour pricks me on. Yea, but how if honour prick me off when I come on? how then? Can honour set-to a leg? No. Or an arm? No. Or take away the grief of a wound? No. Honour hath no skill in surgery, then? No. What is honour? A word. What is that word, honour? Air. A trim reckoning! Who hath it? He that died o'Wednesday. Doth he feel it? No. Doth he hear it? No. It is insensible then? Yea, to the dead. But will it not live with the living? No. Why? Detraction will not suffer it. Therefore I'll none of it: honour is a mere scutcheon: and so ends my catechism.

King Henry the Fourth, Pt 1, Act 5, Sc. 1.

VIRTUE

Virtue? a fig! tis in ourselves that we are thus, or thus. Our bodies are our gardens; to the which our wills are gardeners; so that if we will plant nettles, or sow lettuce; set Hyssop, and weed out thyme; supply it with one gender of herbs, or distract it with many; either to have it sterile with idleness, or manured with industry; why, the power and corrigible authority of this lies in our wills.

Othello, Act 1, Sc. 3.

TO ME, FAIR FRIEND

To me, fair friend, you never can be old,
For as you were when first your eye I ey'd
Such seems your beauty still. Three
winters cold
Have from the forests shook three
summers' pride,
Three beauteous springs to yellow autumn
turn'd
In process of the seasons have I seen,
Three April perfumes in three hot Junes burn'd
Since first I saw you fresh, which yet are green
Ah, yet doth beauty, like a dial-hand,
Steal from his figure, and no pace perceiv'd;
So your sweet hue, which methinks still
doth stand,
Hath motion, and mine eye may be deceiv'd.
For fear of which, hear this, thou age
unbred:
Ere you were born was beauty's
summer dead.

Sonnets, 104.

TRUE LOVE

Let me not to the marriage of true minds
Admit impediments. Love is not love
Which alters when it alteration finds,
Or bends with the remover to remove: –
O no! it is an ever-fixed mark
That looks on tempests, and is never
  shaken;
It is the star to every wandering bark,
Whose worth's unknown, although his
  height be taken.
Love's not Time's fool, though rosy lips
  and cheeks
Within his bending sickle's compass come;
Love alters not with his brief hours and
  weeks,
But bears it out even to the edge of doom:
    If this be error, and upon me proved,
    I never writ, nor no man ever loved.

Sonnets, 116.

GENTLEMEN RECRUITS

Rash, inconsiderate, fiery voluntaries,
With ladies' faces and fierce dragons' spleens,
Have sold their fortunes at their native homes,
Bearing their birthrights proudly on their backs,
To make a hazard of new fortunes here.

King John, Act 3, Sc. 1.

UNEMPLOYMENT

The clothiers all, not able to maintain
The many to them 'longing, have put off
The spinsters, carders, fullers, weavers,
who,
Unfit for other life, compell'd by hunger
And lack of other means, in desperate
manner
Daring the event to the teeth, are all in
uproar,
And danger serves among them.

King Henry the Eighth, Act 1, Sc. 2.

STUDY

Study is like the heaven's glorious sun,
That will not be deep search'd with saucy looks;
Small have continual plodders ever won,
Save base authority from others' books.
These earthly godfathers of heaven's lights,
That give a name to every fixed star,
Have no more profit of their shining nights
Than those that walk and wot not what they are.
Too much to know is to know naught but fame;
And every godfather can give a name.

Love's Labour's Lost, Act 1, Sc. 1.

TRAVEL

Other men, of slender reputation,
Put forth their sons to seek preferment out:
Some to the wars, to try their fortune there;
Some to discover islands far away;
Some to the studious universities.
For any or for all these exercises
He said that Proteus your son was meet,
And did request me to importune you
To let him spend his time no more at home,
Which would be great impeachment to his age,
In having known no travel in his youth.

The Two Gentlemen of Verona, Act 1, Sc. 3.

SHYLOCK'S GRUDGE

How like a fawning publican he looks!
I hate him for he is a Christian:
But more for that, in low simplicity,
He lends out money gratis, and brings
down
The rate of usance here with us in Venice.
If I can catch him once upon the hip,
I will feed fat the ancient grudge I bear
him.
He hates our sacred nation; and he rails,
Even there where merchants most do
congregate,
On me, my bargains, and my well-won
thrift,
Which he calls interest. Cursed be my
tribe,
If I forgive him.

The Merchant of Venice, Act 1, Sc. 3.

SHYLOCK THE JEW

Hath not a Jew eyes? hath not a Jew hands, organs, dimensions, senses, affections, passions? fed with the same food, hurt with the same weapons, subject to the same diseases, healed by the same means, warmed and cooled by the same winter and summer, as a Christian is? If you prick us, do we not bleed? if you tickle us, do we not laugh? if you poison us, do we not die? and if you wrong us, shall we not revenge?

The Merchant of Venice, Act 3, Sc. 1.

BEDLAM BEGGARS

The country gives me proof and precedent,
Of Bedlam beggars, who, with roaring voices,
Strike in their numb'd and mortified bare arms
Pins, wooden pricks, nails, sprigs of rosemary;
And with this horrible object, from low farms,
Poor pelting villages, sheep-cotes and mills
Sometimes with lunatic bans, sometime with prayers,
Enforce their charity.

King Lear, Act 2, Sc. 3.

ROGUERY

They say this town is full of cozenage;
As, nimble jugglers that deceive the eye,
Dark-working sorcerers that change the mind,
Soul-killing witches that deform the body,
Disguised cheaters, prating mountebanks,
And many such-like liberties of sin.

The Comedy of Errors, Act 1, Sc. 2.

GHOSTS

Art thou any thing?
Art thou some god, some angel, or some devil,
That mak'st my blood cold and my hair to stare?
Speak to me what thou art.

Julius Caesar, Act 4, Sc. 3.

WHEN CHURCHYARDS YAWN

'Tis now the very witching time of night;
When churchyards yawn, and hell itself breathes out
Contagion to this world. Now could I drink hot blood,
And do such bitter business as the day
Would quake to look on. Soft; now to my mother.
O, heart, lose not thy nature; let not ever
The soul of Nero enter this firm bosom:
Let me be cruel, not unnatural;
I will speak daggers to her, but use none.

Hamlet, Act 3, Sc. 2.

O GOOD OLD MAN!

O good old man! how well in thee appears
The constant service of the antique world,
When service sweat for duty, not for
  meed!
Thou art not for the fashion of these times,
Where none will sweat but for promotion,
And having that, do choke their service up
Even with the having.

As You Like It, Act 2, Sc. 3.

PORTRAIT OF A MOTHER

Fie, daughter! when my old wife lived,
upon
This day she was both pantler, butler,
cook;
Both dame and servant; welcomed all;
served all;
Would sing her song and dance her turn;
now here,
At upper end o' the table, now i' the
middle;
On his shoulder, and his; her face o'fire
With labour, and the thing she took to
quench it,
She would to each one sip.

The Winter's Tale, Act 4, Sc. 3.

THERE IS A WILLOW

There is a willow grows aslant a brook
That shows his hoar leaves in the glassy
stream.
There with fantastic garlands did she
come,
Of crow-flowers, nettles, daisies, and long
purples
That liberal shepherds give a grosser name
But our cold maids do dead men's fingers
call them.

Hamlet, Act 4, Sc. 7.

WITH FAIREST FLOWERS

Whilst summer lasts, and I live here Fidele,
I'll sweeten thy sad grave; thou shalt not
lack
The flowers that like they face, pale
primrose, nor
The azured harebell, like they veins; no,
nor
The leaf of eglantine, whom not to slander,
Out-sweeten'd not thy breath.

Cymbeline, Act 4, Sc. 2.

FAIRY SONG

Over hill, over dale,
Thorough bush, thorough brier,
Over park, over pale,
Thorough flood, thorough fire,
I do wander everywhere,
Swifter than the moon's sphere;
And I serve the fairy queen,
To dew her orbs upon the green.
The cowslips tall her pensioners be;
In their gold coats spots you see,
Those be rubies, fairy favours,
In those freckles live their savours:
I must go seek some dewdrops here,
And hang a pearl in every cowslip's ear.

A Midsummer Night's Dream, Act 2, Sc. 1.

ARIEL'S SONG

Where the bee sucks, there suck I;
In a cowslip's bell I lie;
There I couch when owls do cry.
On the bat's back I do fly
After summer merrily.
Merrily, merrily shall I live now
Under the blossom that hangs on the
bough.

The Tempest, Act 5, Sc. 1.

HERE'S FLOWERS FOR YOU

Here's flowers for you;
Hot lavender, mints, savory, marjoram.
The marigold, that goes to bed with the sun,
And with him rises weeping; these are flowers
Of middle summer, and I think they are given
To men of middle age.

The Winter's Tale, Act 4, Sc. 4.

THE GARDENER'S ART

Go, bind thou up you dangling apricocks,
Which, like unruly children, make their
sire
Stoop with oppression of their prodigal
weight:
Give some supportance to the bending
twigs.
Go thou, and like an executioner,
Cut off the heads of too fast growing
sprays,
That look too lofty in our commonwealth:
All must be even in our government.
You thus employed, I will go root away
The noisome weeds, that without profit
suck
The soil's fertility from wholesome
flowers.

King Richard the Second, Act 3, Sc. 4.

LOVE'S TRAGEDIES

Ah me! for aught that ever I could read,
Could ever hear by tale or history,
The course of true love never did run
  smooth;
But either it was different in blood,
Or else misgraffed in respect of years,
Or else it stood upon the choice of friends:
Or, if there were a sympathy in choice,
War, death, or sickness did lay siege to it,
Making it momentary as a sound,
Swift as a shadow, short as any dream;
Brief as the lightning in the collied night,
That, in a spleen, unfolds both heaven and
  earth,
And ere a man hath power to say 'Behold!'
The jaws of darkness do devour it up:
So quick bright things come to confusion.

A Midsummer Night's Dream, Act 1, Sc. 1.

LOVE'S IDOLATRY

What you do,
Still betters what is done. When you speak,
sweet,
I'd have you do it ever: when you sing,
I'd have you buy and sell so; so give alms;
Pray so; and, for the ordering your affairs,
To sing them too: when you do dance, I
wish you
A wave o' the sea, that you might ever do
Nothing but that; move still, still so, and
own
No other function: each your doing,
So singular in each particular,
Crowns what you are doing in the present
deeds,
That all your acts are queens.

The Winter's Tale, Act 4, Sc. 4.

THIS ENGLAND

This England never did, nor never shall,
Lie at the proud foot of a conqueror,
But when it first did help to wound itself.
Now these her princes are come home
again,
Come the three corners of the world in
arms,
And we shall shock them: nought shall
make us rue,
If England to itself do rest but true.

King John, Act 5, Sc. 7.

THIS SCEPTER'D ISLE

This royal throne of kings, this scepter'd isle,
This earth of majesty, this seat of Mars,
This other Eden, demi-paradise;
This fortress, built by Nature for herself,
Against infection and the hand of war;
This happy breed of men, this little world;
This precious stone set in the silver sea,
Which serves it in the office of a wall,
Or as a moat defensive to a house,
Against the envy of less happier lands,
England bound in with the triumphant sea,
Whose rocky shore beats back the envious siege
Of watery Neptune, is now bound in with shame,
With inky blots and rotten parchment bonds;
That England, that was wont to conquer others,
Hath made a shameful conquest of itself.

King Richard the Second, Act 2, Sc. 1.

CLEOPATRA'S DREAM OF ANTONY

His legs bestrid the ocean: his rear'd arm
Crested the world: his voice was
  propertied
As all the tuned spheres, and that to
  friends;
But when he meant to quail and shake the
  orb,
He was as rattling thunder. For his bounty,
There was no winter in't; an autumn 'twas,
That grew the more by reaping: his
  delights
Were dolphin-like; they show'd his back
  above
The element they lived in: in his livery
Walk'd crowns and crownets; realms and
  islands were
As plates dropped from his pocket.

Antony and Cleopatra, Act 5, Sc. 2.

O MIGHTY CAESAR!

O mighty Caesar! dost thou lie so low?
Are all thy conquests, glories, triumphs,
  spoils,
Shrunk to this little measure? Fare thee
  well.
I know not, gentlemen, what you intend,
Who else must be let blood, who else is
  rank:
If I myself, there is no hour so fit
As Caesar's death's hour, nor no
  instrument
Of half that worth as those your swords,
  made rich
With the most noble blood of all this
  world.
I do beseech ye, if ye bear me hard,
Now, whilst your purpled hands do reek
  and smoke,
Fulfil your pleasure.

Julius Caesar, Act 3, Sc. 1.

THE NIGHTINGALE

Wilt thou be gone? it is not yet near day:
It was the nightingale, and not the lark,
That pierc'd the fearful hollow of thine
  ear;
Nightly she sings on yon pomegranate
  tree:
Believe me, love, it was the nightingale.

Romeo and Juliet, Act 3, Sc. 5.

WOODLAND BIRDS

'The ousel-cock, so black of hue,
With orange-tawny bill,
The throstle with his note so true,
The wren with little quill.
The finch, the sparrow, and the lark,
The plain-song cuckoo grey,
Whose note full many a man doth mark,
And dares not answer, nay.'

A Midsummer Night's Dream, Act 2, Sc. 1.

INVOCATION TO HARMONY

The web of our life is of a mingled yarn, good and ill together: our virtues would be proud if our faults whipped them not; and our crimes would despair if they were not cherished by our virtues.

All's Well That Ends Well, Act 4, Sc. 3.

THERE IS A TIDE

There is a tide in the affairs of men,
Which, taken at the flood, leads on to
  fortune;
Omitted, all the voyage of their life
Is bound in shallows and in miseries.
On such a full sea are we now afloat;
And we must take the current when it
  serves,
Or lose our ventures.

Julius Caesar, Act 4, Sc. 3.

I KNOW A BANK

I know a bank where the wild thyme
  blows,
Where oxlips and the nodding violet
  grows;
Quite over-canopied with luscious
  woodbine,
With sweet musk-roses, and with
  eglantine.
There sleeps Titania, sometime of the
  night,
Lull'd in these flowers with dances and
  delight.

A Midsummer Night's Dream, Act 2, Sc. 1.

WOODLAND SOLITUDE

. . . unfrequented woods,
I better brook than flourishing peopled towns,
Here can I sit alone, unseen of any,
And to the nightingale's complaining notes,
Tune my distresses, and record my woes.

The Two Gentlemen of Verona, Act 5, Sc. 4.

LOVE'S WONDER

O! she doth teach the torches to burn
bright.
It seems she hangs upon the cheek of night
Like a rich jewel in an Ethiop's ear;
Beauty too rich for use, for earth too dear!
So shows a snowy dove trooping with
crows,
As yonder lady o'er her fellows shows.
The measure done, I'll watch her place of
stand,
And, touching hers, make blessed my rude
hand.
Did my heart love till now? forswear it,
sight!
For I ne'er saw true beauty till this night.

Romeo and Juliet, Act 1, Sc. 5.

LOVE'S DANGERS

As love is full of unbefitting strains;
All wanton as a child, skipping and vain;
Form'd by the eye, and, therefore, like the
eye,
Full of stray shapes, of habits and of forms,
Varying in subjects, as the eye doth roll
To every varied object in his glance.

Love's Labour's Lost, Act 5, Sc. 2.

WAR

Now all the youth of England are on fire,
And silken dalliance in the wardrobe lies;
Now thrive the armourers, and honour's
  thought
Reigns solely in the breast of every man:
They sell the pasture now to buy the horse,
Following the mirror of all Christian kings,
With winged heels, as English Mercuries.
For now sits Expectation in the air
And hides a sword from hilts unto the
  point
With crowns imperial, crowns and
  coronets,
Promis'd to Harry and his followers.

King Henry the Fifth, Act 2, Prologue.

THE DEVASTATION OF WAR

And all her husbandry doth lie on
heaps,
Corrupting in its own fertility.
Her vine, the merry cheerer of the heart,
Unpruned dies; her hedges even-pleached,
Like prisoners, wildly overgrown with
hair,
Put forth disordered twigs; her fallow leas,
The darnel, hemlock, and rank fumitory,
Doth root upon, while that the coulter
rusts,
That should deracinate such savagery.

King Henry the Fifth, Act 5, Sc. 2.

THE WOMAN'S PART

Could I find out
The woman's part in me! For there's no motion
That tends to vice in man but I affirm
It is the woman's part; be it lying, note it,
The woman's; flattering, hers; deceiving, hers;
Lust and rank thoughts, hers, hers; revenges, hers;
Ambitions, coveting, change of prides, disdain,
Nice longing, slanders, mutability,
All faults that man may name, nay, that hell knows,
Why, hers, in part, or all; but rather, all.

Cymbeline, Act 2, Sc. 5.

FRAILTY OF WOMEN

Fie, fie upon her!
There's language in her eye, her cheek, her lip,
Nay, her foot speaks; her wanton spirits look out
At every joint and motive of her body.
O, these encounterers, so glib of tongue,
That give a coasting welcome ere it comes,
And wide unclasp the tables of their thoughts
To every ticklish reader! Set them down
For sluttish spoils of opportunity
And daughters of the game.

Troilus and Cressida, Act 4, Sc. 5.

THE VINEYARD

He hath a garden circummur'd with brick,
Whose western side is with a vineyard
back'd
And to that vineyard is a planched gate,
That makes his opening with this bigger
key;
This other doth command a little door,
Which from the vineyard to the garden
leads.

Measure for Measure, Act 4, Sc. 1.

THE PLEACHED BOWER

Bid her steal into the pleached bower,
Where honeysuckles ripen'd by the sun,
Forbid the sun to enter; like favourites,
Made proud by princes, that advance their pride
Against that power that bred it.

Much Ado About Nothing, Act 3, Sc. 1.

THE RAGING STORM

Blow, winds, and crack your cheeks! rage!
  blow!
You cataracts and hurricanoes, spout
Till you have drench'd our steeples,
  drown'd the cocks!
You sulphurous and thought-executing
  fires,
Vaunt-couriers to oak-cleaving
  thunderbolts,
Singe my white head! And thou,
  all-shaking thunder,
Strike flat the thick rotundity o' the world!
Crack nature's moulds, all germens spill at
  once
That make ingrateful man!

King Lear, Act 3, Sc. 2.

COME, LET'S AWAY

Come, Let's away to prison;
We two alone will sing like birds i' the cage:
When thou dost ask me blessing, I'll kneel down
And ask of thee forgiveness: so we'll live,
And pray, and sing, and tell old tales, and laugh
At gilded butterflies, and hear poor rogues
Talk of court news; and we'll talk with them too,
Who loses and who wins; who's in, who's out;
And take upon's the mystery of things,
As if we were God's spies; and we'll wear out,
In a wall'd prison, packs and sets of great ones
That ebb and flow by the moon.

King Lear, Act 5, Sc. 3.

FESTE'S SONG

Come away, come away, death,
And in sad cypress let me be laid:
Fly away, fly away, breath,
I am slain by a fair cruel maid.
My shroud of white, stuck all with yew,
O prepare it!
My part of death, no one so true
Did share it.

Not a flower, not a flower sweet,
On my black coffin let there be strown;
Not a friend, not a friend greet
My poor corpse, where my bones shall be thrown.
A thousand, thousand sighs to save,
Lay me, O, where
Sad true lover never find my grave,
To weep there!

Twelfth Night, Act 2, Sc. 4.

DESDEMONA'S SONG

The poor soul sat sighing by a sycamore
 tree;
  Sing all a green willow:
Her hand on her bosom, her head on her
 knee,
  Sing willow, willow, willow.
The fresh streams ran by her, and
 murmur'd her moans,
  Sing willow, willow, willow.
Her salt tears fell from her, and soften'd
 the stones,
  Sing willow, willow, willow.
Sing all a green willow must be my
 garland:
Let nobody blame him, his scorn I approve.
I called my love false love, but what said
 he then?
  Sing willow, willow, willow.
If I court moe women, you'll couch with
 moe men.

Othello, Act 4, Sc. 3.

GRIEF

Grief fills the room up of my absent child,
Lies in his bed, walks up and down with
me,
Puts on his pretty looks, repeats his words,
Remembers me of all his gracious parts,
Stuffs out his vacant garments with his
form;
Then have I reason to be fond of grief.
Fare you well: had you such a loss as I,
I could give better comfort than you do.
I will not keep this form upon my head,
When there is such disorder in my wit.
O Lord! my boy, my Arthur, my fair son!
My life, my joy, my food, my all the
world!
My widow-comfort, and my sorrows'
cure!

King John, Act 3, Sc. 4.

DEATH'S TRIUMPH

No longer mourn for me when I am dead
Than you shall hear the surly sullen bell
Give warning to the world that I am fled
From this vile world, with vilest worms to
dwell.
Nay, if you read this line, remember not
The hand that writ it; for I love you so,
That I in your sweet thoughts would be
forgot,
If thinking on me then should make you
woe.
O if, I say, you look upon this verse,
When I perhaps compounded am with
clay,
Do not so much as my poor name rehearse
But let your love even with my life decay;
Lest the wise world should look into
your moan,
And mock you with me after I am
gone.

Sonnets, 71.

LOVER'S CHOICE

Why, that's the lady: all the world desires
  her;
From the four corners of the earth they
  come,
To kiss this shrine, this mortal-breathing
  saint:
The Hyrcanian deserts and the vasty wilds
Of wide Arabia are as thoroughfares now
For princes to come view fair Portia.

The Merchant of Venice, Act 2, Sc. 7.

LOVER'S TEST

Before thee stands this fair Hesperides,
With golden fruit, but dangerous to be
touch'd;
For death-like dragons here affright thee
hard:
Her face, like heaven, enticeth thee to view
Her countless glory, which desert must
gain;
And which, without desert, because thine
eye
Presumes to reach, all thy whole heap must
die.

Pericles, Act 1, Sc. 1.

PASTORAL SYMPHONY

Ceres, most bounteous lady, thy rich leas
Of wheat, rye, barley, vetches, oats, and peas;
Thy turfy mountains, where live nibbling
  sheep,
And flat meads thatch'd with stover, them
  to keep;
Thy banks with pioned and twilled brims,
Which spongy April at thy hest betrims,
To make cold nymphs chaste crowns;
  and thy broom groves
Whose shadow the dismissed bachelor loves,
Being lass-lorn; thy pole-clipt vineyard;
And thy sea-marge, sterile and rocky-hard,
Where thou thyself dost air: the queen o' the sky,
Whose watery arch and messenger am I,
Bids thee leave these; and with her
  sovereign grace,
Here on this grass-plot, in this very place,
To come and sport; her peacocks fly amain:
Approach, rich Ceres, her to entertain.

The Tempest, Act 4, Sc. 1.

BOUNTEOUS NATURE

Why should you want? Behold, the earth
  hath roots;
Within this mile break forth a hundred
  springs;
The oaks bear mast, the briers scarlet hips;
The bounteous housewife, nature, on each
  bush
Lays her full mess before you.

Timon of Athens, Act 4, Sc. 3.

Earth's increase, foison plenty,
Barns and garners never empty,
Vines with clust'ring bunches growing,
Plants with goodly burden bowing;
Spring come to you at the farthest
In the very end of harvest!

The Tempest, Act 4, Sc. 1.

MY NATIVE ENGLISH

The language I have learn'd these forty
  years,
My native English, I must now forego;
And now my tongue's use is to me no
  more
Than an unstringed viol or a harp,
Or like a cunning instrument cas'd up,
Or, being open, put into his hands
That knows no touch to tune the harmony.

King Richard the Second, Act 1, Sc. 3.

WOLSEY'S FAREWELL

So farewell to the little good you bear me.
Farewell! a long farewell, to all my
greatness!
This is the state of man: today he puts forth
The tender leaves of hopes; to-morrow
blossoms,
And bears his blushing honours thick upon
him;
The third day comes a frost, a killing frost;
And, when he thinks, good easy man,
full surely
His greatness is a-ripening, nips his root,
And then he falls, as I do. I have ventur'd
Like little wanton boys that swim on bladders,
This many summers in a sea of glory,
But far beyond my depth: my high-blown pride
At length broke under me, and now has left me,
Weary and old with service, to the mercy
Of a rude stream, that must for ever hide me.

King Henry the Eighth, Act 3, Sc. 2.

NATURE'S FOREBODING

The night has been unruly: where we lay,
Our chimneys were blown down; and,
as they say,
Lamenting heard i' the air; strange screams
of death,
And prophesying with accents terrible
Of dire combustion and confus'd events
New hatch'd to the woeful time. The
obscure bird
Clamour'd the livelong night: some say
the earth
Was feverous and did shake.

Macbeth, Act 2, Sc. 3.

WARNING OF DISASTER

In the most high and palmy state of Rome,
A little ere the mightiest Julius fell,
The graves stood tenantless and the sheeted
  dead
Did squeak and gibber in the Roman
  streets;
As stars with trains of fire and dews of
  blood,
Disasters in the sun; and the moist star
Upon whose influence Neptune's empire
  stands
Was sick almost to doomsday with eclipse.

Hamlet, Act 1, Sc. 1.

THE MURMURING STREAM

The current that with gentle murmur
glides,
Thou know'st, being stopp'd,
impatiently doth rage;
But when his fair course is not hindered,
He makes sweet music with th' enamell'd
stones,
Giving a gentle kiss to every sedge
He overtaketh in his pilgrimage;
And so by many winding nooks he strays
With willing sport, to the wild ocean.

The Two Gentleman of Verona, Act 2, Sc. 7.

WOODLAND SOLITUDE

Hath not old custom made this life more sweet
Than that of painted pomp? Are not these woods
More free from peril than the envious court?
Here feel we but the penalty of Adam,
The seasons' difference; as, the icy fang
And churlish chiding of the winter's wind,
Which, when it bites and blows upon my body,
Even till I shrink with cold, I smile and say,
'This is no flattery.'

As You Like It, Act 2, Sc. 1.

HARK! HARK! THE LARK

Hark! hark! the lark at heaven's gate sings,
    And Phoebus 'gins arise,
His steeds to water at those springs
    On chaliced flowers that lies;
And winking Mary-buds begin
    To ope their golden eyes:
With everything that pretty bin,
    My lady sweet, arise!
        Arise, arise!

Cymbeline, Act 2, Sc. 3.

SILVIA

Who is Silvia? What is she,
    That all our swains commend her?
Holy, fair, and wise is she;
    The heaven such grace did lend her,
That she might admired be.

Is she kind as she is fair?
    For beauty lives with kindness.
Love doth to her eyes repair,
    To help him of his blindness;
And, being helped, inhabits there.

Then to Silvia let us sing,
    That Silvia is excelling;
She excels each mortal thing,
    Upon the dull earth dwelling:
To her let us garlands bring.

The Two Gentlemen of Verona, Act 4, Sc. 2.

TO BE, OR NOT TO BE

To be, or not to be; that is the question:
Whether 'tis nobler in the mind to suffer
The slings and arrows of outrageous
  fortune,
Or to take arms against a sea of troubles,
And by opposing end them? To die, to
  sleep;
No more; and, by a sleep to say we end
The heart-ache and the thousand natural
  shocks
That flesh is heir to, 'tis a consummation
Devoutly to be wish'd. To die, to sleep;
To sleep: perchance to dream; ay, there's
  the rub;
For in that sleep of death what dreams
  may come
When we have shuffled off this mortal coil,
Must give us pause.

Hamlet, Act 3, Sc. 1.

CONTENTMENT

O God! methinks it were a happy life,
To be no better than a homely swain;
To sit upon a hill, as I do now,
To carve out dials, quaintly, point by
  point,
Thereby to see the minutes how they run,
How many make the hour full complete;
How many hours bring about the day;
How many days will finish up the year;
How many years a mortal man may live.

King Henry the Sixth, Pt. 3, Act 2, Sc. 5.

ARCHERY

In my schooldays, when I had lost one
shaft,
I shot his fellow of the self-same flight
The self-same way, with more advised
watch,
To find the other forth; and by adventuring
both
I oft found both.

The Merchant of Venice, Act 1, Sc. 1.

CALIBAN

I'll show thee the best springs; I'll pluck thee berries;
I'll fish for thee, and get thee wood enough.
A plague upon the tyrant that I serve!
I'll bear him no more sticks, but follow thee,
Thou wondrous man.
I pr'y thee, let me bring thee where crabs grow:
And I with my long nails will dig thee pig-nuts:
Show thee a jay's nest, and instruct thee how
To snare the nimble marmozet; I'll bring thee
To clustering filberds, and sometimes I'll get thee
Young sea-mells from the rock.

The Tempest, Act 2, Sc. 2.

CORIN

I know, the more one sickens, the worse at ease he is; and that he that wants money, means, and content, is without three good friends: – That the property of rain is to wet, and fire to burn: That good pasture makes fat sheep: and that a great cause of the night is lack of the sun: That he, that hath learned no wit by nature nor by art, may complain of good breeding, or comes of a very dull kindred.

As You Like It, Act 3, Sc. 2.

DAN CUPID

This wimpled, whining, purblind,
  wayward boy,
This senior-junior, giant-dwarf, Dan
  Cupid;
Regent of love rhymes, lord of folded
  arms,
The anointed sovereign of sighs and
  groans,
Liege of all loiterers and malcontents.

Love's Labour's Lost, Act 3, Sc. 1.

A SOLDIER TELLS

Her father lov'd me; oft invited me;
Still question'd me the story of my life
From year to year, the battles, sieges,
 fortunes
That I have pass'd.
I ran it through, even from my boyish
 days
To the very moment that he bade me tell
 it . . . This to hear
Would Desdemona seriously incline;
But still the house-affairs would draw her
 thence;
Which ever as she could with haste
 dispatch,
She'd come again, and with a greedy ear
Devour up my discourse . . .
She lov'd me for the dangers I had pass'd,
And I lov'd her that she did pity them.

Othello, Act 1, Sc. 3.

PROLOGUE

But pardon, gentles all,
The flat unraised spirits that hath dar'd
On this unworthy scaffold to bring forth
So great an object: can this cockpit hold
The vasty fields of France? or may we cram
Within this wooden O the very casques
That did affright the air at Agincourt?
Piece out our imperfections with your
thoughts:
Into a thousand parts divide one man,
And make imaginary puissance;
Think when we talk of horses that you see
them
Printing their proud hoofs i' the receiving earth;
For 'tis your thoughts that now must deck
our kings,
Carry them here and there, jumping o'er
times,
Turning the accomplishment of many years
Into an hour-glass.

King Henry the Fifth, Prologue.

FRIENDSHIP

Friendship is constant in all other things,
Save in the office and affairs of love:
Therefore all hearts in love use their own
  tongues;
Let every eye negotiate for itself,
And trust no agent; for beauty is a witch,
Against whose charms faith melteth into
  blood.

Much Ado About Nothing, Act 2, Sc. 1.

REPUTATION

Good name in man and woman, dear my
  lord,
Is the immediate jewel of their souls:
Who steals my purse steals trash; 'tis
  something, nothing;
'Twas mine, 'tis his, and has been slave to
  thousands;
But he that filches from me my good name
Robs me of that which not enriches him,
And makes me poor indeed.

Othello, Act 3, Sc. 3.

THE FOOD OF LOVE

If music be the food of love, play on;
Give me excess of it, that, surfeiting,
The appetite may sicken, and so die.
That strain again! it had a dying fall:
O! it came o'er my ear like the sweet
  sound
That breathes upon a bank of violets,
Stealing and giving odour. Enough! no
  more:
'Tis not so sweet now as it was before.
O spirit of love! how quick and fresh art
  thou,
That, notwithstanding thy capacity
Receiveth as the sea, nought enters there,
Of what validity and pitch soe'er,
But falls into abatement and low price,
Even in a minute: so full of shapes is fancy,
That it alone is high fantastical.

Twelfth Night, Act 1, Sc. 1.

LOVE'S SUFFERING

To be in love, where scorn is bought with groans;
Coy looks with heart-sore sighs; one fading moment's mirth
With twenty watchful, weary, tedious nights:
If haply won, perhaps a hapless gain;
If lost, why then a grievous labour won:
However, but a folly bought with wit,
Or else a wit by folly vanquished.

The Two Gentlemen of Verona, Act 1, Sc. 1.

THE FEAR OF DEATH

Ay, but to die, and go we know not where;
To lie in cold obstruction and to rot;
This sensible warm motion to become
A kneaded clod; and the delighted spirit
To bathe in fiery floods, or to reside
In thrilling region of thick-ribbed ice;
To be imprison'd in the viewless winds,
And blown with restless violence round
  about
The pendant worlds; or to be worse than
  worst
Of those that lawless and uncertain
  thoughts
Imagine howling: 'tis too horrible!
The weariest and most loathed worldly life
That age, ache, penury and imprisonment
Can lay on nature is a paradise
To what we fear of death.

Measure for Measure, Act 3, Sc. 1.

O, AMIABLE LOVELY DEATH

Death, death: O, amiable lovely death!
Thou odiferous stench! sound rottenness!
Arise forth from the couch of lasting night,
Thou hate and terror to prosperity,
And I will kiss thy detestable bones,
And put my eyeballs in thy vaulty brows,
And ring these fingers with thy household
  worms,
And stop this gap of breath with fulsome
  dust,
And be a carrion monster like thyself:
Come, grin on me; and I will think thou
  smil'st
And buss thee as thy wife! Misery's love,
O! come to me.

King John, Act 3, Sc. 4.

THE MAGIC ISLE

Be not afeard: the isle is full of noises,
Sounds and sweet airs, that give delight,
and hurt not.
Sometimes a thousand twangling
instruments
Will hum about my ears; and sometime
voices,
That, if I then had wak'd after long sleep,
Will make me sleep again: and then, in
dreaming,
The clouds methought would open and
show riches
Ready to drop upon me; that, when I
wak'd
I cried to dream again.

The Tempest, Act 3, Sc. 3.

QUEEN MAB

She is the fairies' midwife, and she comes
In shape no bigger than an agate-stone
On the fore-finger of an alderman,
Drawn with a team of little atomies
Over men's noses as they lie asleep;
Her wagon-spokes made of long spinners' legs.
The cover of the wings of grasshoppers,
Her traces of the smallest spider web,
Her collars of the moonshine's watery beams,
Her whip of cricket's bone, the lash of film,
Her wagoner a small grey-coated gnat,
Not half so big as a round little worm
Prick'd from the lazy finger of a maid;
Her chariot is an empty hazel-nut
Made by the joiner squirrel, or old grub,
Time out o' mind the fairies' coachmakers.

Romeo and Juliet, Act 1, Sc. 4.

ANGLING

The pleasant'st angling is to see the fish
Cut with her golden oars the silver stream,
And greedily devour the treacherous bait;

Much Ado About Nothing, Act 3, Sc. 1.

Words more sweet, and yet more
  dangerous,
Than baits to fish.

Titus Andronicus, Act 4, Sc. 6.

The tender nibbler would not touch the
  bait.

Passionate Pilgrim, verse IV, line 11.

She knew her distance, and did angle for
  me;

All's Well That Ends Well, Act 5, Sc. 3.

THE ART OF SWIMMING

I saw him beat the surges under him,
And ride upon their backs: he trod the
  water
Whose enmity he flung aside, and breasted
The surge most swoln that met him: his
  bold head
'Bove the contentious waves he kept, and
  oar'd
Himself with his good arms in lusty stroke
To the shore.

The Tempest, Act 2, Sc. 1.

THE POPINJAY

But I remember, when the fight was done,
When I was dry with rage and extreme
  toil,
Breathless and faint, leaning upon my
  sword,
Came there a certain lord, neat, and trimly
  drest,
Fresh as a bridegroom; and his chin new
  reapt
Show'd like a stubble-land at harvest-
  home;
He was perfumed like a milliner;
And 'twixt his finger and his thumb he
  held
A pouncet-box, which ever and anon
He gave his nose, and took't away again.

Henry the Fourth, Pt 1, Act 1, Sc. 3.

WIGS

Look on beauty,
And you shall see 'tis purchas'd by the weight;
So are those crisped snaky golden locks
Which make such wanton gambols with the wind,
Upon supposed fairness, often known
To be the dowry of a second head,
The skull that bred them, in the sepulchre.

The Merchant of Venice, Act 3, Sc. 2.

ABSENCE

How like a winter hath my absence been
From thee, the pleasure of the fleeting year!
What freezings have I felt, what dark days seen!
What old December's bareness every where!
And yet this time remov'd was summer's time;
The teeming autumn, big with rich increase,
Bearing the wanton burden of the prime,
Like widow'd wombs after their lords' decrease.
Yet this abundant issue seem'd to me
But hope of orphans and unfather'd fruit;
For summer and his pleasures wait on thee,
And, thou away, the very birds are mute;
Or, if they sing, 'tis with so dull a cheer,
That leaves look pale, dreading the winter's near.

Sonnets, 97.

WHEN IN DISGRACE

When in disgrace with fortune and men's eyes
I all alone beweep my outcast state,
And trouble deaf heaven with my bootless cries,
And look upon myself and curse my fate,
Wishing me like to one more rich in hope,
Featured like him, like him with friends possess'd,
Desiring this man's art and that man's scope,
With what I most enjoy contented least;
Yet in these thoughts myself almost despising,
Haply I think on thee – and then my state,
Like to the lark at break of day arising
From sullen earth, sings hymns at heaven's gate;
For thy sweet love remember'd such wealth brings
That then I scorn to change my state with kings.

Sonnets, 29.

CURSE ON A THANKLESS CHILD

Hear, nature, hear! dear goddess hear!
Suspend thy purpose, if thou didst intend
To make this creature fruitful!
Into her womb convey sterility!
Dry up in her the organs of increase,
And from her derogate body never spring
A babe to honour her! If she must teem,
Create her child of spleen, that it may live
And be a thwart disnatur'd torment to her!
Let it stamp wrinkles in her brow of youth,
With cadent tears fret channels in her
  cheeks,
Turn all her mother's pains and benefits
To laughter and contempt, that she may
  feel
How sharper than a serpent's tooth it is
To have a thankless child!

King Lear, Act 1, Sc. 4.

DOVER CLIFF

How fearful and dizzy 'tis to cast one's
  eyes so low!
The crows and choughs that wing the
  midway air
Show scarce so gross as beetles; half way
  down
Hangs one that gathers samphire, dreadful
  trade!
Methinks he seems no bigger than his head.
The fishermen that walk upon the beach
Appear like mice, and yond tall anchoring
  bark
Diminished to her cock, her cock a buoy
Almost too small for sight. The
  murmuring surge,
That on the unnumber'd idle pebbles
  chafes,
Cannot be heard so high. I'll look no more,
Lest my brain turn, and the deficient sight
Topple down headlong.

King Lear, Act 4, Sc. 6.

THE HONEY BEES

For so work the honey bees,
Creatures that by a rule in nature teach
The act of order to a peopled kingdom.
They have a king and officers of sorts:
Where some like magistrates correct at
home,
Others like merchants venture trade
abroad;
Others like soldiers armed in their stings
Make boot upon the summer's velvet buds.

King Henry the Fifth, Act 1, Sc. 2.

THE HUNT

The hunt is up, the morn is bright and
grey,
The fields are fragrant and the woods are
green:
Uncouple here and let us make a bay,
And wake the emperor and his lovely
bride,
And rouse the prince and ring a hunter's
peal,
That all the court may echo with the noise.

Titus Andronicus, Act 2, Sc. 2.

But go with speed
To some forlorn and naked hermitage,
Remote from all the pleasures of the world;
There stay, until the twelve celestial signs
Have brought about their annual reckoning.
If this austere insociable life
Change not your offer made in heat of blood;
If frosts and fasts, hard lodging and thin weeds,
Nip not the gaudy blossoms of your love,
But that it bear this trial and last love;
Then, at the expiration of the year,
Come challenge me, challenge me by these deserts,
And, by this virgin palm now kissing thine,
I will be thine.

Love's Labour's Lost, Act 5, Sc. 2.

ADVICE

Give thy thoughts no tongue,
Nor any unproportion'd thought his act.
Be thou familiar, but by no means vulgar;
The friends thou hast, and their adoption
tried,
Grapple them to thy soul with hoops of
steel;
But do not dull thy palm with
entertainment
Of each new-hatch'd, unfledg'd comrade.
Beware
Of entrance to a quarrel, but, being in,
Bear't that th' opposed may beware of
thee.
Give every man thine ear, but few thy
voice;
Take each man's censure, but reserve thy
judgment.

Hamlet, Act 1, Sc. 3.

THE BLAST OF WAR

But when the blast of war blows in our ears,
Then imitate the action of the tiger: . . .
Then lend the eye a terrible aspect; . . .
Now set the teeth and stretch the nostril wide,
Hold hard the breath and bend up every spirit
To his full height! On, on, you noblest English

King Henry the Fifth, Act 3, Sc. 1.

ESCAPE

My lord, our army is dispers'd already:
Like youthful steers unyok'd, they take
their courses
East, west, north, south; or, like a school
broke-up,
Each hurries to his home and sporting-
place.

King Henry the Fourth, Pt 2, Act 4, Sc. 2.

THE BURDEN OF KINGSHIP

How many thousand of my poorest subjects
Are at this hour asleep! O sleep! O gentle sleep!
Nature's soft nurse, how have I frighted thee,
That thou no more wilt weigh my eyelids down
And steep my senses in forgetfulness?
Why rather, sleep, liest thou in smoky cribs,
Upon uneasy pallets stretching thee,
And hush'd with buzzing night-flies to thy slumber,
Than in the perfum'd chambers of the great,
Under the canopies of costly state,
And lull'd with sound of sweetest melody?
O thou dull god! why liest thou with the vile
In loathsome beds, and leav'st the kingly couch
A watch-case or a common 'larum bell?

King Henry the Fourth, Pt 2, Act 3, Sc. 1.

RECONCILIATION

England hath long been mad, and scarr'd herself;
The brother blindly shed the brother's blood,
The father rashly slaughter'd his own son,
The son, compell'd, been butcher to the sire:
All this divided York and Lancaster,
Divided in their dire division,
O! now, let Richmond and Elizabeth,
The true succeeders of each royal house,
By God's fair ordinance conjoin together;
And let their heirs, – God, if thy will be so, –
Enrich the time to come with smooth-fac'd peace,
With smiling plenty, and fair prosperous days!

King Richard the Third, Act 5, Sc. 4.

A WIFE'S DUTY

A woman mov'd is like a fountain troubled,
Muddy, ill-seeming, thick, bereft of beauty;
And while it is so, none so dry or thirsty
Will deign to sip or touch one drop of it.
Thy husband is thy lord, thy life, thy keeper,
They head, thy sovereign; one that cares for thee,
And for thy maintenance commits his body
To painful labour both by sea and land,
To watch the night in storms, the day in cold,
Whilst thou liest warm at home, secure and safe;
And craves no other tribute at thy hands
But love, fair looks, and true obedience;
Too little payment for so great a debt.

The Taming of the Shrew, Act 5, Sc. 2.

SIGH NO MORE

Sigh no more, ladies, sigh no more,
Men were deceivers ever;
One foot in sea, and one on shore,
To one thing constant never.
Then sigh not so,
But let them go,
And be you blithe and bonny!
Converting all your sounds of woe
Into Hey nonny, nonny.

Sing no more ditties, sing no moe,
Of dumps so dull and heavy;
The fraud of men was ever so,
Since summer first was leavy.
Then sigh not so,
But let them go,
And be you blithe and bonny;
Converting all your sounds of woe
Into Hey nonny, nonny.

Much Ado About Nothing, Act 2, Sc. 3.

TO HIS LOVE

When in the chronicle of wasted time
I see descriptions of the fairest wights,
And beauty making beautiful old rhyme
In praise of ladies dead, and lovely knights;
Then in the blazon of sweet beauty's best
Of hand, of foot, of lip, of eye, of brow,
I see their antique pen would have exprest
Ev'n such a beauty as you master now.
So all their praises are but prophecies
Of this our time, all, you prefiguring;
And for they look'd but with divining
  eyes,
They had not skill enough your worth to
  sing:
    For we, which now behold these
      present days,
    Have eyes to wonder, but lack tongues
      to praise.

Sonnets, 18.

LOVE'S HERALDS

Love's heralds should be thoughts,
Which ten times faster glide than the sun's beams,
Driving back shadows over low'ring hills:
Therefore do nimble-pinion'd doves draw Love,
And therefore hath the wind-swift Cupid wings.

Romeo and Juliet, Act 2, Sc. 5.

THE CHOICE

Whether, if you yield not to your father's choice,
You can endure the livery of a nun,
For aye to be in shady cloister mew'd,
To live a barren sister all your life,
Chanting faint hymns to the cold fruitless moon.
Thrice blessed they that master so their blood,
To undergo such maiden pilgrimage;
But earthlier happy is the rose distill'd,
Than that which withering on the virgin thorn
Grows, lives, and dies, in single blessedness.

A Midsummer Night's Dream, Act 1, Sc. 1.

HOW SWEET THE MOONLIGHT

How sweet the moonlight sleeps upon this
bank!
Here will we sit, and let the sounds of
music
Creep in our ears: soft stillness and the
night
Become the touches of sweet harmony.
Sit, Jessica: look, how the floor of heaven
Is thick inlaid with patines of bright gold:
There's not the smallest orb which thou
behold'st
But in his motion like an angel sings,
Still quiring to the young-eyed cherubins;
Such harmony is in immortal souls.

The Merchant of Venice, Act 5, Sc. 1.

INNOCENCE

We were as twinn'd lambs that did frisk i'
the sun,
And bleat the one at the other: what we
chang'd
Was innocence for innocence; we knew
not
The doctrine of ill-doing, no nor dream'd
That any did. Had we pursu'd that life,
And our weak spirits ne'er been higher
rear'd
With stronger blood, we should have
answer'd heaven
Boldly, 'not guilty'; the imposition clear'd
Hereditary ours.

The Winter's Tale, Act 1, Sc. 2.

THE SLEEPING IMOGEN

The crickets sing, and man's o'erlabour'd
sense
Repairs itself by rest. Our Tarquin thus
Did softly press the rushes ere he waken'd
The chastity he wounded. Cytherea,
How bravely thou becom'st thy bed! fresh
lily,
And whiter than the sheets! That I might
touch!
But kiss: one kiss! Rubies unparagon'd,
How dearly they do't! 'Tis her breathing
that
Perfumes the chamber thus; the flame of
the taper
Bows toward her, and would under-peep
her lids,
To see the enclosed lights, now canopied
Under these windows, white and azure
lac'd
With blue of heaven's own tinct.

Cymbeline, Act 2, Sc. 2.

NOBLE BRUTUS

This was the noblest Roman of them all;
All the conspirators save only he
Did that they did in envy of great Caesar;
He only, in a general honest thought
And common good to all, made one of them.
His life was gentle, and the elements
So mix'd in him that Nature might stand up
And say to all the world, 'This was a man!'

Julius Caesar, Act 5, Sc. 5.

CASSIUS ON CAESAR

Why, man, he doth bestride the narrow
  world
Like a Colossus; and we petty men
Walk under his huge legs, and peep about
To find ourselves dishonourable graves.
Men at some time are masters of their
  fates:
The fault, dear Brutus, is not in our stars,
But in ourselves, that we are underlings.

Julius Caesar, Act 1, Sc. 2.

UNDER THE GREENWOOD TREE

Under the greenwood tree
Who loves to lie with me,
And tune his merry note
Unto the sweet bird's throat –
Come hither, come hither, come hither!
        Here shall he see
        No enemy
But winter and rough weather.

Who doth ambition shun
And loves to live i' the sun,
Seeking the food he eats
And pleased with what he gets –
Come hither, come hither, come hither!
        Here shall he see
        No enemy
But winter and rough weather.

As You Like It, Act 2, Sc. 5.

WINTER

When icicles hang by the wall,
And Dick the shepherd blows his nail,
And Tom bears logs into the hall,
And milk comes frozen home in pail,
When blood is nipp'd, and ways be foul,
Then nightly sings the staring owl:
'Tu-who;
Tu-whit, Tu-who' – A merry note,
While greasy Joan doth keel the pot.

When all aloud the wind doth blow,
And coughing drowns the parson's saw,
And birds sit brooding in the snow,
And Marian's nose looks red and raw,
When roasted crabs hiss in the bowl,
Then nightly sings the staring owl:
'Tu-who;
Tu-whit, To-who' – A merry note,
While greasy Joan doth keel the pot.

Love's Labour's Lost, Act 5, Sc. 2.

A BEDCHAMBER

It was hang'd
With tapestry of silk and silver; the story
Proud Cleopatra, when she met her
Roman,
. . . a piece of work
So bravely done, so rich, that it did strive
In workmanship and value; . . . and the
chimney-piece
Chaste Dian bathing; never saw I figures
So likely to report themselves . . .
. . . The roof o' the chamber
With golden cherubins is fretted; her
andirons . . .
. . . were two winking Cupids
Of silver.

Cymbeline, Act 2, Sc. 4.

SLEEPING BEAUTY

Without the bed her other fair hand was,
On the green coverlet; whose perfect white
Show'd like an April daisy on the grass,
With pearly sweat, resembling dew of
night,
Her eyes, like marigolds, had sheath'd
their light
And canopied in darkness sweetly lay,
Till they might open to adorn the day.

Lucrece, verse 57.

GOLD

'Tis gold
Which buys admittance; oft it doth; yea, and makes
Diana's rangers false themselves, yield up
Their deer to the stand of the stealer; and 'tis gold
Which makes the true man kill'd, and saves the thief;
Nay, sometime hangs both thief and true man: what
Can it not do and undo?

Cymbeline, Act 2, Sc. 3.

TO GILD REFINED GOLD

To gild refined gold, to paint the lily,
To throw a perfume on the violet,
To smooth the ice, or add another hue
Unto the rainbow, or with taper light
To seek the beauteous eye of heaven to
  garnish,
Is wasteful and ridiculous excess.

King John Act 4, Sc. 2.

THE WHEEL OF FORTUNE

Nay, then farewell!
I have touch'd the highest point of all my
greatness;
And from that full meridian of my glory,
I haste now to my setting: I shall fall
Like a bright exhalation in the evening,
And no man see me more.

King Henry the Eighth, Act 3, Sc. 2.

LIFE'S PHILOSOPHY

To-morrow, and to-morrow, and to-
morrow,
Creeps in this petty pace from day to day,
To the last syllable of recorded time;
And all our yesterdays have lighted fools
The way to dusty death. Out, out, brief
candle!
Life's but a walking shadow, a poor player
That struts and frets his hour upon the
stage
And then is heard no more; it is a tale
Told by an idiot, full of sound and fury,
Signifying nothing.

Macbeth, Act 5, Sc. 5.

WE ARE SUCH STUFF

Our revels now are ended. These our
actors,
As I foretold you, were all spirits and
Are melted into air, into thin air:
And, like the baseless fabric of this vision,
The cloud-capp'd towers, the gorgeous
palaces,
The solemn temples, the great globe itself,
Yea, all which it inherit, shall dissolve
And, like this insubstantial pageant faded,
Leave not a rack behind. We are such stuff
As dreams are made on, and our little life
Is rounded with a sleep.

The Tempest, Act 4, Sc. 1.